DID YOU KNOW?
Kea

DID YOU KNOW?
Kea
young
reed

Contents

What is a Kea?

- Kea are **birds** belonging to the **parrot** family, so their relatives include the likes of cockatoos, macaws and budgerigars.
- Just like other birds they have **feathers** and a **beak** and **lay eggs** in a nest from which their young hatch.
- They are highly intelligent and **social**, often **hanging out in pairs or small groups**.

Facts and figures

- The Kea is about **forty centimetres long** from the tip of its beak to the tip of its tail. When standing up it is about the **same size as a pet cat.**
- Adapted to life in **harsh mountain environments** – with strong winds, cold temperatures and frequent snow – Kea are **strong fliers** and **very hardy.**

- These clever parrots have been known to use tools such as sticks to help them get their food.
- Kea have been recorded to live for at least thirty years.

Special adaptations

- A Kea's long pointed beak is used for digging out food, such as roots from the earth and insect grubs from rotten logs.

- The bright reds in their plumage are thanks to special pigments called psittacofulvins. Only parrots can produce these.

- Feathers keep the birds warm by trapping a layer of air underneath. Like all birds they keep their feathers in pristine condition by preening and oiling them using a special oil gland above the tail.

- Parrots need to eat bits of grit to help them squash up and digest the food in their stomach.

Special pigments produce the bright red colours.

Regular bathing helps keep the feathers in good condition.

Eating grit helps with digestion.

Preening.

Kea and people

- Kea are very inquisitive birds and they are fascinated by humans and aspects of human life such as cars and buildings.

- Sometimes their interest is not so welcome, for example they have a habit of stealing windscreen wipers from cars and eating the rubber!

- They can also be destructive by chewing other structures such as aerials on cars and buildings.
- Raiding rucksacks and picnic baskets is another of their tricks.

Where do they live?

- Kea live only in the **Southern Alps**, which run down the length of the South Island of **New Zealand**. They are found nowhere else in the world.

- Some live high in the mountains, at altitudes of up to **two thousand metres** above sea level.

- As the tree line is at around nine hundred metres, many Kea live on barren rocky slopes, making it the world's only alpine parrot species.

Closest relatives

- Kea are related to the world's other four hundred or so parrot species.

Kākā.

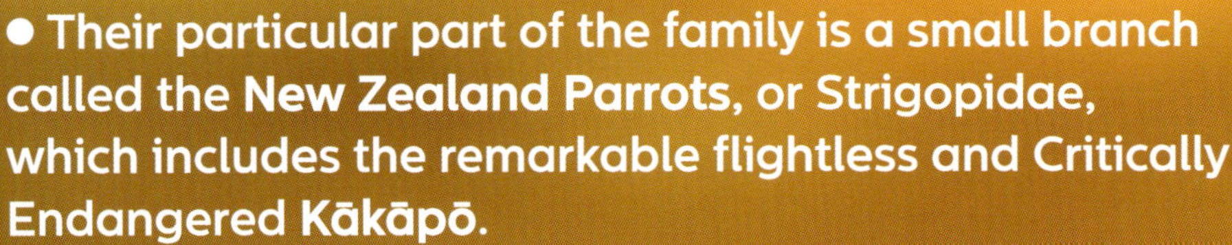

- Their particular part of the family is a small branch called the **New Zealand Parrots**, or Strigopidae, which includes the remarkable flightless and Critically Endangered **Kākāpō**.

- The Kea's closest relative is the **Kākā**, which is found widely on North, South and Stewart Islands in New Zealand, where it likes to live in **forests** in more **lowland** areas. The Kākā can be easily distinguished from the Kea thanks to its **redder plumage**.

Kea.

Kākāpō.

Life in the nest

- Kea make their **nest in a hole** – either a burrow in the ground or a hollow in a tree trunk or log, or among rocks.
- The female lays and incubates **two to four white eggs**, while the male brings food for the female.

- White fluffy babies emerge from the eggs after **three weeks**.

● The young birds spend a further **three months** growing up in the nest before they are ready to leave and make their way in the wider world.

Although Kea often approach people for a free handout, it is best not to feed them as human food can be harmful to these birds.

What's for dinner?

- Kea are omnivores and opportunist feeders, meaning that they will feed on just about anything.
- They eat fruit, nectar, roots and other parts of plants.

- Insects and their larvae also feature in the Kea's diet.
- They are also partial to meat, taking reptiles, young birds and carrion (dead animals – yuck!).

Threats to Kea

- With fewer than **seven thousand birds remaining** today, the Kea is listed as **Threatened** internationally and considered **Nationally Endangered** by the New Zealand government.

- **Humans are their main threat.** Between 1860 and 1970 **one hundred and fifty thousand** Kea were hunted and killed with the encouragement of farmers and the support of the government.

- Today **hunting is banned** and **the species is protected.**

- Kea still fall victim to road-traffic accidents and are killed by non-native predators introduced by people, such as **feral cats** and **stoats**, while **possums** and **rats** will prey on the eggs and young.

Stoat.

Feral cat.

First published in 2025 by
New Holland Publishers

newhollandpublishers.com

A record of this book is held at the National Library of Australia.

ISBN 9781760798062

OTHER TITLES IN THE 'DID YOU KNOW?' SERIES:

Capybara
ISBN 9781760798048

Dolphins
ISBN 9781921078000

Kangaroos
ISBN 9781921073861

Kiwi
ISBN 9781760798079

Koala
ISBN 9781921073878

Lizards
ISBN 9781921073885

Meerkat
ISBN 9781921073892

Penguins
ISBN 9781921073908

Red Panda
ISBN 9781921073915

For details of these books and hundreds of other Natural History titles see newhollandpublishers.com